RESTAURANT MANAGER'S POCKET HANDBOOK

LABOR COST

25 KEYS TO

Profitable Success

DAVID V. PAVESIC, F.M.P.

Copyright© 1999 by David V. Pavesic, Ph.D.
Lebhar-Friedman Books

Lebhar-Friedman Books is a company of Lebhar-Friedman Inc.

Printed in the United States of America

Library of Congress Cataloging-in-Publication Data

Pavesic, David V.
    Restaurant manager's pocket handbook : 25 keys to
    profitable success. Labor cost / David V. Pavesic.
        p.   cm.
    Includes index.
    ISBN 0-86730-753-6 (pbk.)
    1. Restaurants--Cost control.   2. Labor costs.   I. Title.
    TX911.3.C65P388   1998
    647.95'0681--dc21   98-39299
                                                             CIP

LABOR ISSUES are probably the chief concern of all restaurant owners and managers. There simply are not enough qualified applicants for the positions we need to fill. We struggle with high turnover and seek to find ways to retain employees just a little longer. Our industry continues to be identified with minimum-wage jobs, long hours, and insufficient benefits.

Labor costs are not controlled by paying low wages; they are controlled through scheduling and improving employee productivity. Productivity is increased through training, better kitchen and dining-room layouts, and the use of labor-saving equipment and products. However, even with those technological advances, gains in productivity are negated by the high turnover and low retention rate of employees in the foodservice industry.

Those fundamental problems have been characteristic of the hospitality industry for years. But rather than working collectively as owners and operators to change the environment for the "health" of our workers, we look for employees who are willing to work under those conditions. And until we change the environment, we will continue to turn off many qualified and productive employees in the labor pool.

This handbook doesn't cover those human resource issues, as that topic would require a volume of its own. In this book we explore cost-related issues and ways to measure productivity and the importance of scheduling in controlling labor costs. The reporting of labor-related figures also is discussed. Before you can develop appropriate and effective measures for labor-cost control, you must possess the necessary information to make those decisions. Therefore, the accumulation and reporting of relevant labor-cost information is critical.

Productivity and labor-cost efficiency are not addressed and assessed only in quantitative terms. A low payroll percentage or a high customer-per-labor-hour index may at first appear to be a positive sign. However, one cannot lose sight of the qualitative side of the activity. If customer service is compromised, the initial savings of a lower payroll can be negated by a decrease in sales caused by customer defections to competitors.

Employees cannot be viewed and treated as "inputs" without feelings, needs, and fears. Every time the industry is faced with a labor shortage, such as the one we have today, it "gets religion" and becomes more empathetic to the needs of its employees. That is accompanied by a temporary shift away from a bottom-line mentality to one emphasizing human relations. Just remember: The two most important groups of individuals affecting your business's success are your customers and your employees. Both must be treated in the same way.

24... If you reduce employee turnover and increase retention, productivity will improve.   **PAGE 85**

25... Once labor costs have been cut to the bare bones, only an increase in sales can lower the payroll percentage.   **PAGE 87**

The traditional ratio of payroll to total sales is not an effective and accurate measure of worker productivity and scheduling efficiency

THE PRIMARY INDEX used by management to evaluate labor cost is the ratio of total payroll to total sales. It is not the best indicator of scheduling efficiency and worker productivity. Three reasons explain why additional measures must be used to analyze labor costs.

First, the traditional labor-cost ratio is an aggregate figure that is far too general to provide specific information on what areas must be addressed. Typically, the monthly income statement shows the payroll for the entire month as a single figure. Because it is a composite of wages from employees in all job categories — servers, cooks, dishwashers, etc. — it's impossible to determine from the percentage which category is the cause of the variance from standard cost. Furthermore, it doesn't tell management during which meal period or day of the week the greatest variance occurred.

Second, the figures reported on the monthly income statement are historical and after-the-fact. Even if the completed statement is reviewed by management the first week of the following month, nothing can be done about what occurred in the past. Labor cost must be precontrolled. That requires that labor-cost figures be compiled at least weekly and, preferably, daily.

Third, the payroll percentage is distorted by increases and decreases in sales. When business is good, the percentage of payroll to sales is low. When sales are low, the opposite occurs. The decrease or increase in the percentage isn't always an indication that labor productivity has risen or fallen; it is partly caused by the large fixed-cost component of payroll. In addition, the percentage can be distorted further by increases in menu prices, wage-rate increases, discount promotions, and shifts in the menu-sales mix.

No single measure can be used to evaluate labor productivity; management must employ multiple measures collectively

MANAGEMENT MUST HAVE a more effective index of labor productivity than the traditional labor-cost percentage. Additional measures are required to analyze labor costs properly. The additional information required is readily available and easily compiled on a daily or weekly basis in most restaurants. Those measures are *covers per labor hour, labor cost per hour, and labor cost per cover.*

Each time payroll is processed, total labor hours by job category is tallied. Management will compare actual hours worked with those originally scheduled and note any variances. If hours worked are significantly greater or less than scheduled hours, management will investigate to determine the job category and the time of day in which the variance occurred.

Employee schedules are determined, not

> **"Knowledge is a candle lighted in the mind and left alight."**
>
> — ANONYMOUS

so much by the sales levels as by customer counts, or covers. Covers per labor hour are perhaps the most inflation-proof indicator of labor productivity because it's not distorted by sales that have been affected by price increases or discounts. Although some decrease in customer counts may occur over time when prices are increased, covers per labor hour remains the most effective indicator of employee productivity. The number of covers per labor hour are calculated for each job category and for the entire payroll by dividing total labor hours by the customer count.

Labor cost per labor hour is another productivity index that relies on the cover count and is calculated by dividing total payroll by total labor hours. When that measure is calculated for each employee job category, one can readily see the wage differentials between jobs — information that can assist management in establishing wage ranges for each job category.

The third index of productivity is the labor cost per cover, a measure that tells us how much labor is used to serve each customer. To calculate that figure, the total payroll is divided by the number of customers. Analysis of that index by job category typically will reveal a rather wide cost spread between categories like hostess/cashiers, servers, and cooks. The averages within each job category are skewed by the number of employees, the average hourly wages, and the number of hours worked. For example, two hostesses will be scheduled for a busy meal period that requires 12 to 16 servers; consequently, the job categories with the fewest number of employees scheduled will show the highest cover per labor hour.

The calculations for each of the three indexes are as follows:

Assume that the total payroll cost is $1,400; total labor hours are 200; and the total number of covers served are 1,500.

- To calculate the covers per labor hour, divide 1,500 by 200, which equals 7.5.

- To arrive at the labor cost per labor hour, divide $1,400 by 200, which equals $7.

- To determine the labor cost per cover, divide $1,400 by 1,500, which equals 93 cents.

(1) Labor costs can be brought under control by paying the minimum acceptable wages in your market area.

    A. True
    B. False

(2) The ratio of labor cost to total sales is the best indicator of scheduling efficiency and worker productivity.

    A. True
    B. False

(3) Which of the following are deficiencies of the traditional labor-cost ratio found on most restaurant income statements?

    A. Is too general to provide management with specific information on where costs are out of line
    B. Come too late to be of real value in pre-controlling labor costs
    C. None of the above

(4) Which of the following measures is the weakest indicator for assessing scheduling efficiency and worker productivity?

    A. Covers per labor hour
    B. Average check per cover
    C. Labor cost per labor hour

(5) Increases in prices and hourly wages can distort the traditional labor cost percentage.

    A. True
    B. False

ANSWERS: 1: B, 2: B, 3: C, 4: B, 5: A

Sales per labor hour and average check are not good indicators of labor productivity

SEVERAL REASONS unrelated to productivity can explain the differences in average check and sales per labor hour. Employing sales per labor hour — which is calculated by dividing sales revenue by total labor hours worked — is only marginally better than the aggregate labor cost percentage. Many fast-food operations use sales per labor hour as a tool to scheduling. For example, if one employee could be scheduled for every $25 in hourly sales and a $125 hour was forecasted, as many as five labor hours would be allowed during that hour.

    If the operation's sales per labor hour met or exceeded that standard, the manager has scheduled efficiently. But that method has several weaknesses that must be noted. First, whenever menu prices are increased, that index will appear to improve without any scheduling

"Nothing great was ever achieved without enthusiasm."

— RALPH WALDO EMERSON

changes. Second, many fast-food operations with drive-through windows that schedule workers according to that index have found they were short-handed during breakfast and lunch hours. Two reasons can be cited for that. In the first place the average check per transaction is lower at breakfast; therefore, to achieve $25 in sales, a greater number of transactions are required. Second, workers should be scheduled according to the number of customers/transactions anticipated, not according to sales revenue. Drive-through windows can increase the number of transactions that are served in an hour, requiring additional employees to be scheduled.

In some cases sales per labor hour actually can decrease, even after menu prices are increased. That doesn't necessarily signal lower productivity because many restaurants extend their operations into the late-night and early-morning hours to maximize the use of the building and equipment. In operations open 24 hours, skeleton crews must be on hand during the early hours when business is so slow that even a skeleton crew cannot meet productivity standards. Sales per labor hour also are lowered because of the hiring of inexperienced part-time workers whose productivity is generally lower until they have been trained properly.

The calculations for those indexes are as follows:

> Assume that the number of labor hours is 200; the cover count is 1,500; and sales are $15,000.

> - To calculate sales per labor hour, divide $15,000 by 200. The answer is $75.
> - To determine average check, divide $15,000 by 1,500, which equals $10.

Average check is also subject to variances not directly related to employee productivity. In the case of restaurants with identical menus and prices but different locations, the menu-sales mix and the demographics of the clientele could be the reason for the differences. Assume one location is in a resort area where the primary customers are tourists, while the other is in a residential area. Tourists tend to spend freely, while residents will "shop" for best meal bargains during the work week. It wouldn't be surprising to find that the average check is lower at the unit in the residential area and higher at the outlet in the resort area. Consequently, average check and sales per labor hour must be interpreted with those things in mind.

(1) When sales per labor hour is used to schedule employees, you could be under-staffed for meal periods such as breakfast when the average transaction is much less than it is at lunch or dinner.

    A. True
    B. False

(2) A restaurant's location can have a signifi-cant impact on the average check per cus-tomer.

    A. True
    B. False

(3) Productivity and labor-cost efficiency are only addressed in "quantitative" terms.

    A. True
    B. False

(4) Which of the following conditions con-tribute to the high turnover of employees in the restaurant industry?

    A. Low hourly rate of pay
    B. Long hours
    C. All of the above

(5) The accumulation and reporting of relevant labor-cost information is critical to controlling labor.

    A. True
    B. False

ANSWERS: 1: A, 2: A, 3: B, 4: C, 5: A

Realistic productivity standards must be established for each job category

A STANDARD IS A GOAL or expected level of performance that becomes the benchmark you will compare with the actual performance. It's an ideal condition one wishes to attain and a sense of where one seeks to be in relation to where one actually is at a point in time. The process of establishing realistic productivity standards begins with assembling data on productivity, which requires planning on the part of management.

Before attempting to develop any standard of employee performance or productivity, you must possess a clear and detailed perspective of the operation. That involves defining quality standards for food and beverages, the level of customer service, and the demographics of the customer base.

Once the products and services to be offered have been described, it will become

> **"I don't know the key to success, but the key to failure is to try to please everyone."**
>
> — BILL COSBY

---

apparent which jobs need to be filled and the skill levels required. The regular assignment of work can be ascertained and schedules developed. You must conduct that analysis for your own operation; industry standards or those of a competitor will not work for your operation. Review schedules and hours worked for each employee-job category. Break down the information by days of the week and meal periods. Observe employees on the job and grade their productive efforts throughout their shift.

Observation of workers in action will enable you to identify the employees with the best and poorest productivity. The most productive employees serve as the *standard of productivity* for that position. An efficient measurement must be made of both the amount of work that must be accomplished within a time frame and the number of employees who are required to accomplish that work at the minimum qualitative level of performance. Those activity levels become the standards of performance for manpower requirements for each job classification.

Ask such questions as, "What makes an efficient cook or dishwasher?" "What is it that makes Tom a more productive cook than Bill?" "How many covers can Tom handle before he needs help?" In essence, what you're conducting is a form of work analysis utilized by human-resource engineers to determine the number of workers needed at the different levels of business activity. The number required will depend on the quantitative output and the qualitative standards expected.

That information serves both as a basis for writing job descriptions and establishing staffing guidelines. It also may reveal inefficiencies and opportunities for including labor-saving equipment, present a better way to arrange the work center, identify time-saving equipment and utensils, and even target those tasks that could be accomplished by another employee or job category.

Standards must be established based on actual on-the-job conditions and not measurements in a controlled environment. Each standard must be general enough to account for the varying abilities of employees and actual circumstances of the task and work environment.

(1) Labor-cost standards can be universally applied across the foodservice industry.
   A. True
   B. False

(2) A standard is a goal or expected level of performance that is compared to actual performance or results.
   A. True
   B. False

(3) Only the "quantitative" level of performance is factored into performance standards.
   A. True
   B. False

(4) Standards must be established based on actual on-the-job conditions to be truly effective.
   A. True
   B. False

(5) The activity levels of your most productive employees can serve as your standard of performance for each job classifications.
   A. True
   B. False

ANSWERS: 1: B, 2: A, 3: B, 4: A, 5: A

If you want your employees to be productive, you must invest in them

IN ORDER FOR PRODUCTIVITY to improve, employees must be properly and adequately trained — and that costs money. Neither productivity nor quality of service can improve without the investment of time and resources in employee training. Get used to the fact that there will always be an insufficient number of qualified applicants for each position.

Hiring the "best of the applicants" doesn't mean you hired correctly. When demand for workers exceeds the supply of qualified applicants, management often resorts to the rationale of hiring the "best" applicants, even when they don't meet the minimal qualifications for the position. It's easy to see how that can happen after operating shorthanded for several weeks.

Country-western comedian Jerry Clower tells a story about a hunter climbing a tree to

> **"The important thing to recognize is that it takes a team, and the team ought to get credit for the wins and the losses. Successes have many fathers; failures have none."**
>
> — PHILIP CALDWELL

---

knock down what he thought was a raccoon, only to discover that his dogs had treed a bobcat. A terrible commotion ensues up in the tree with fur and clothing raining down. The hunter yells to his friend on the ground to shoot the bobcat because it's tearing him up. The friend replies that he's afraid he might accidentally shoot the hunter instead. To which the man in the tree says, "Just shoot amongst both of us because one of us has got to have some relief." Well, the cure may be worse than the disease when we find ourselves with employees who can't really do the job at the qualitative and quantitative levels we'd like. We sacrifice our standards just to fill the position.

Labor-cost savings result from increasing retention and increasing productivity. The solution that addresses both retention and productivity is training. If productivity can be improved, fewer employees can accomplish more. The one irrefutable fact of the restaurant industry is that we hire many employees at the minimum wage, and many of our entry-level workers are unskilled. The tenure of those employees with any single operator is so short that it's not deemed cost effective to spend much on training and development. As a result, we create a self-fulfilling prophecy of low productivity and high turnover. That cycle is difficult to break and is looked upon as a fact of life in the industry.

It follows that if you have poor hiring practices, you will have greater employee turnover and higher-than-average labor costs. And it's a basic principle of management that states if you hire unskilled employees, you must train them to be productive.

If you don't invest in training, another fundamental management principle states that you must provide adequate supervision. That's another area where we as managers fall down. Inadequate supervision of unskilled employees further exacerbates the self-fulfilling prophecy of low productivity and high turnover. The span of control — or the number of employees under the control of one supervisor — is reduced if employees aren't trained and skilled. In an effort to decrease administrative costs, many chains are reducing the number of district and regional supervisors that regularly called upon their location managers. That can work if unit managers are adequately trained and qualified. However, many employees have been promoted to management positions for which they were not qualified — they were the "best" of the applicant pool. Without adequate supervi-

sion it will take longer for them to become productive, and they will have to learn through trial
and error.

We complain that employees today have
poor work habits and a bad attitude. We expect
them to come to us already trained and motivated. Without adequate training and supervision, it's hardly surprising that we get low productivity, bad service, waste, and inefficiency in
our operations. Both management and hourly
workers experience stress working in that kind
of environment. You must budget adequately
for the training and supervision of your employees if you expect them to be productive.

You cannot control labor cost until you understand that you are not scheduling people, but rather purchasing the potential to do work

MANY MANAGERS SCHEDULE more staffers than are necessary because they're afraid of being short-handed. If the anticipated increase in business doesn't materialize, and everyone who has been scheduled shows up, productivity declines. The only conceivable reason for scheduling an additional employee is that certain work must be done, and that person can do the job. While many operators are feeling the effects of the short supply of quality applicants, the scheduling of employees within their payroll budget is sometimes contrary to their ability to sustain service quality.

The cost of employing a worker is far greater than his or her total net pay, regardless of whether the worker is salaried or hourly. Labor cost can be defined as any cost incurred as a result of employing a worker. You can estimate that an employee's total remuneration, deferred or otherwise, is at least double his or her earnings before taxes. Additional costs of employing a worker include such fringe benefits as insurance, paid vacations, profit sharing, uniforms, meals, training costs, discounts and retirement plans.

You must resist the temptation to "panic hire." Panic hiring occurs when you've been working short-handed for several weeks, and the applicant pool doesn't possess the qualifications you require. However, you haven't had a day off in three weeks, and you're fearful that other employees who have been working overtime are thinking about quitting themselves. So, in desperation you hire the "best" of the applicants you've interviewed rather than hold out for the right person. But by doing that you could end up creating more problems than if you had worked through the problem until you were able to find the kind of employee you really needed.

Don't force your employees to choose between their jobs and their personal lives

WHEN I STARTED OUT in this business back in the 1960s, most managers and owners came up through the ranks, or "the school of hard knocks," as they called it. I remember one interview I had with the president of a restaurant company when I was in my early 20s. I was teaching at a junior college in Kansas City, Mo., and needed a summer job. The vice president of the company had set up the interview and apparently had given me a recommendation that didn't match my age and appearance. When I walked into the president's office, he did a double take. Then he turned to the vice president and said: "This can't be the guy you told me about. He's too young to know everything you said, and he doesn't have gray hair."

I told him I was, in fact, the same guy, and that some day I would have gray hair. I knew

> **"Uncertainty will always be a part of the taking-charge process."**
>
> — HAROLD GENEEN

early in the interview that I was not going to get the job. My education was working against me. The president told me how he started off as dishwasher and never went to college; feasibility studies were a waste of time; and he made most decisions based on "a gut feeling," not theories in books. He also told me he worked 70 to 80 hours a week, and he had 20 years of experience, not just four years of college.

Reflecting back on that experience, I can come up will all kinds of clever rebuttals to his remarks. But at the time I just listened respectfully and thanked him when it was over. Today we know that experience is no longer enough to succeed, and that you cannot go on only "a gut feeling" — especially when a sizable financial investment and the lives of dozens of people ride on the results of your decision. I wonder how many self-made managers really have just one year of experience and 19 years of repetition of what they learned that first year.

My point is that while you may have had to work 70 to 80 hours a week to get to where you are today, these are different times. Today's employees "work to live," and do not "live to work." They place greater importance on their families, friends, and personal lives; they want and need time to enjoy life along the way. Get used to the fact that they will make more money than you did at their age, have more time off, and experience the good life long before you did — and before you think they've earned it. You probably were viewed the same way by your employer when you started.

One more thing: Quality-of-life issues are important to both management and hourly personnel. Even employees with a workaholic mentality can burn out. They need time away from the business on a regular basis to keep their edge and drive.

When demand for labor exceeds the supply of applicants, management softens its approach to employee relations. Good employees are shown appreciation and respect. Management wants to retain them and is willing to increase their pay and benefits and give them time off when they require it. But all too often that occurs when a valued employee turns in his or her notice. Management asks why he or she is leaving, and often the reason has nothing to do with money. More often than not it has to do with quality-of-life issues.

Administrators and owners must understand that a manager, cook, or server requires "quality time" away from the pressures of the workplace. The more responsibility an employee takes on, the more stress he or she is likely to be under. Today, neither men nor women feel that it's fair when their job forces them to subordinate their family responsibilities and social life to the demands of their employer. It's especially difficult to accept in the hospitality industry where the hours are long and the pay is low.

A recent college graduate was hired for a management position, and after several months without more than one day off per week, she suddenly realized that her social life had ground to a complete halt. Is it so difficult to understand why she — and so many others like her — decide to quit their jobs and even get out of the industry within the first five years? When a bottom-line mentality drives the management philosophy, wages are not increased, staffing is reduced, increased demands are placed on those employees who remain, and quality-of-life concerns are discounted by top management.

The message being sent to employees is that they must adapt to a workaholic lifestyle if they expect to be successful and advance in their careers. The foodservice industry continues to lose many good people every year. Furthermore, the environment is turning off potential employees. Certainly, some individuals around can deal with long hours, low pay, and high stress. But fewer of those types exist today than 25 years ago.

The greatest portion of your labor cost is a fixed expense

IF YOU DIVIDE YOUR PAYROLL into fixed- and variable-cost labor, you probably will discover that the largest portion is fixed. The fixed-cost portion of payroll isn't just management salaries that must be paid regardless of sales volume; it's also the hourly employees you need to schedule during the slowest hours, meal periods, and days of the week. It's your skeleton crew or the bare-bones staff you must have to open your doors, even when sales revenues fall to their lowest levels. It can only decrease if you ask management and other employees to do more than one job. At this point labor cannot be reduced further without lowering your standards.

The employees who are added to the fixed schedule as business increases are your variable-cost employees. Few restaurants schedule an entire shift to arrive at the same time. Staffers arrive in half-hour intervals, and schedules are staggered to correspond to the arrival of customers. On busy nights additional servers, bussers, and kitchen staff are scheduled to handle the increased volume of business. Having too many variable-cost employees on the schedule raises payroll percentages over standard costs.

Labor cost doesn't increase proportionally to sales increases. An increase of 50 customers an hour might require one or two more servers to be added to the schedule, while other job categories would remain constant. Additional bartenders or hostesses might not be added to the schedule until customer counts increase by 100. Consequently, payroll cost increases in incremental steps, not in direct proportion to sales.

As customer counts reach their maximum and the restaurant is on a wait, the maximum number of employees is scheduled. No additional employees are added because productivity can't be increased at that point, and staffers even may get in each other's way. Technically, labor cost is fixed at the maximum and the minimum business volume. However, unless the restaurant normally opens to a wait and remains in that condition until closing, scheduling will include both fixed- and variable-cost employees.

Administrators and unit managers evaluate labor costs differently

THERE IS AN ONGOING DIALOGUE between top managers and operations management concerning labor-cost standards. Top management closely monitors the ratio of payroll-to-sales and tends to be critical of unit managers when that percentage increases. On the other hand, unit managers will contend that the service quality provided the customer is equally important to income and profits.

During periods when sales are up and labor-cost percentages are down, top management becomes less concerned with the number of employees scheduled by unit mangers. But when labor costs are high, top management knows that the only ways to reduce labor costs is to cut back on the schedule or increase sales. The danger of scheduling cutbacks is that it also may reduce the level of service.

Both levels of management must have common criteria for assessing the efficiency and productivity of manpower resources and for analyzing labor costs. That measure must reflect both the qualitative and quantitative aspects of labor cost and customer service. The different perspectives on labor cost held by administrators and operations management must be balanced in both cost containment and the ability to deliver quality service. Top management seeks to keep labor costs contained, while operations management must schedule an adequate number of employees to sustain service standards.

If an operation is expected to have productive employees who consistently can deliver the level of service that provides a competitive edge over the competition, adequate training and supervision must be available. Providing quality service and having productive employees involves a cost. Therefore, before labor costs can decrease and employees become more productive, expect your labor costs to increase.

Establish a reporting and evaluation system to monitor labor cost

ANALYSIS OF LABOR COST begins with the assembly of data and its organization in a format that can be interpreted readily by management. Without cost data there can be no analysis. The data required are already assembled in your payroll and sales reports; however, they must be compiled into a format that enables you to see the relationships between the numbers.

When customer counts are broken down by meal periods and days of the week and then cross-referenced with labor hours, sales revenues, and payroll costs, the format will reveal the days, meal periods, and job categories that are not within your standards.

The measurement criteria used to for analyzing labor productivity must be held constant over time. If the criteria are changed, comparisons of current data with historical records will

> **"If you're not serving the customer, you'd better be serving someone who is."**
>
> — KARL ALBRECHT

---

be misleading. For example, you must define clearly what constitutes "one cover" — the single inflation-proof criterion used in scheduling and labor-cost productivity analysis. Do you count small children? Do you count adults who don't order a full breakfast? Do you count "seats" or "orders"? What you do is your decision. The key is to count customers in a consistent manner.

A coffee shop in a motel decided after several years to stop counting morning coffee-only customers. That gave the impression that customer counts were down about 20 percent. As a result, the historical breakfast customer counts became relatively useless. What the coffee shop should have done was to count coffee-only customers separately but keep a tally of them so that overall customer counts could be compared.

Any cost-analysis system requires that standards of scheduling be based on forecasts of customer counts over the payroll period. Typically, forecasts should be made for a 10-day to two-week span. The time frame should correspond to your restaurant's payroll period. The heart of the labor analysis is the measurement of actual labor hours and customer counts compared with forecasted figures.

Organizing weekly payroll dates into a format that allows you to see how payroll costs are broken down will improve your insight into controlling labor cost. The comparison of current figures with those of past periods will indicate where variances in labor-cost standards are occurring. Total aggregate figures by themselves will not provide the details necessary for cost analysis. By monitoring the labor cost per cover by job category, you can determine quickly where overscheduling has occurred.

To illustrate how payroll data is organized into a format conducive to in-depth analysis, the following payroll worksheet has been supplied. (*See next page.*) Figures are shown separately for food and beverage employees. Food sales are $12,000, and food customers are 1,600. Beverage sales are $4,500, and beverage customers are 850.

One can quickly see where the majority of labor cost and labor hours is located. Comparison of actual hours worked with hours scheduled will reveal the amount of additional payroll cost incurred.

FOOD DEPARTMENT	Servers	Bussers	Dishers	Cooks	Hostess	TOTALS
Payroll	$455.10	$338.10	$196.00	$882.00	$168.00	$2,039.20*
Labor hours	222	98	56	168	42	586
% of labor hours	37.9%	16.7%	9.5%	7.2%	7.2%	100.0%
Labor cost %	3.8%	2.8%	1.6%	7.4%	1.4%	17.0%
% of payroll	22.3%	16.6%	9.6%	43.3%	8.2%	100.0%
Cost/labor hours	$2.05	$3.45	$3.50	$5.25	$4.00	$3.48 avg.
Sales/labor hours	$54.05	$122.45	$214.29	$71.43	$285.71	$20.48 avg.
Covers/labor hours	7.2	16.3	28.6	9.5	38.1	2.7
Labor cost/cover	$.28	$.21	$.12	$.55	$.105	$1.27 avg.

*Management salaries not included

BEVERAGE DEPARTMENT	Bartenders	Cocktail waitresses	TOTALS
Payroll	$280.00	$245.00	$525.00
Labor hours	56	98	154
% of labor hours	36.4%	63.6%	100.0%
Labor cost %	6.2%	5.4%	11.6%
% of payroll	53.3%	46.7%	10.0%
Cost/labor hour	$5.00	$2.50	$3.41 average
Sales/labor hour	$80.36	$45.92	$29.22 average
Covers/labor hour	15.2	8.7	5.5 average
Labor cost/cover	$.33	$.29	$.62

(1) Hiring the "best" applicant does not mean you have hired correctly.

    A. True
    B. False

(2) Poor hiring practices lead to greater employee turnover, lower productivity, and higher-than-average labor costs.

    A. True
    B. False

(3) Customer service always is better when a restaurant is overstaffed for the volume of business.

    A. True
    B. False

(4) The largest portion of your labor cost expense is "fixed" as opposed to "variable."

    A. True
    B. False

(5) The amount you spend for labor increases proportionally with your sales increases.

    A. True
    B. False

ANSWERS: 1: A, 2: A, 3: B, 4: A, 5: B

11

KEY

Labor cost must be precontrolled

THE BEST TIME TO CONTROL labor cost is *in advance*. The key to advance control lies in efficient scheduling, and efficient scheduling requires an understanding of the quantitative and qualitative aspects of each job category and the forecasted level of business activity. One cannot forecast without knowledge of what transpired in the past and the conditions which impacted the sales activity.

Once labor cost has been incurred, it cannot be lowered or recovered. If you were overstaffed yesterday, you cannot recover the cost by understaffing tomorrow. Therefore, you must schedule only the amount of labor hours needed for the forecasted volume of business activity.

Precontrol implies advance planning compared with after-the-fact corrective action. One seeks to maximize profits first, as opposed to minimizing losses after the damage has occurred. The comparison of data from past periods with current and forecasted figures is important in precontrolling labor cost. The essence of precontrolling is knowing where you're going, not where you've been.

A data base is necessary if one expects to precontrol labor cost. The data stored in point-of-sale registers must be compiled immediately and reported to management. Summary reports are printed as often as management requires them. The faster management is apprised of negative variances or trends, the faster management can take remedial action.

The comparison of actual data with forecasts is the critical step in locating trouble areas in the employee schedule. It won't tell you exactly what has occurred or why; that must be determined by closely examining the conditions. However, the first step in correcting a problem is discovering that there is one! Precontrol allows management to prepare daily and weekly schedules that will optimize the use of labor while providing the quality and quantity aspects of worker productivity.

Payroll data must be reviewed as frequently as sales and purchases, not just every pay period. When labor costs are excessive, many operators will take readings on labor hours every meal period. A minimum period of two months is recommended before forecasting labor-hour requirements can be accurate. As time goes by and the historical data base increases, the forecasting of customer counts becomes more accurate, making it much easier to schedule for the demand.

KEY

*Labor cost is controlled
through scheduling
techniques, not by paying
low salaries and hourly
wages*

YOU CAN'T CONTROL LABOR COST by keeping
salaries and wages low. In fact, operations paying less than the going wage rate find it difficult
to hire and retain the more productive employees. Think about it. If you were a good bartender, cook, or manager, would you quit your
current job to work for someone who paid you
less than you already are making? I don't think
many of us would work for less.

It's not unusual to find low productivity
and inefficiency in an operation where low
wages are paid relative to other operations of
its type in the immediate area. A low wage
scale usually will attract marginal employees
whose efficiency, work ethic, and temperament
disqualify them from landing identical positions
in restaurant companies paying above-average
wages to above-average applicants. The good

LABOR COST • 47

> **"In business for yourself, not by yourself."**
>
> — RAY KROC

---

employees will go where they're equitably compensated for their skills and abilities.

A regional fried-chicken operator seeking to sell franchises asked me to help him develop a franchisee manual. When I examined his job categories and wage rates, I discovered that the highest-paid hourly employees were making only 10 cents to 20 cents per hour more than the starting hourly rate. When I inquired about it, I was told that employees quit when they weren't given raises, but that didn't concern the manager because he could just hire someone else at a lower rate. The operator believed that paying lower wages was a way to control payroll.

Approximately one-third of all employees who leave a job voluntarily leave for better pay. You may have heard that money can't be used as a motivator for increasing productivity. Well, it's probably true that simply increasing an employee's wages won't necessarily make him more productive. But when money is used as a reward for outstanding performance, it can send a strong message.

A number of scheduling methodologies are available that you can use to reduce labor costs just by adjusting arrival and departure times for employees. Efficient scheduling must reflect the variations in business volume that occur during the day and evening meal periods. The goal is to accomplish the necessary work load with a minimum number of labor hours while maintaining your level of service.

Productive employees should be rewarded with pay increases so that they earn more than average employees. Treat your valuable employees as you do your most valuable customers. Understand that the labor cost per cover and the number of covers per labor hour can be improved only with productive employees. If productive employees are treated no differently than marginally productive ones, the good employees won't feel motivated to do any more than an average amount of work.

(1) Precontrol of labor cost requires one to forecast the expected level of business activity.

   A. True
   B. False

(2) Payroll data does not need to be reviewed as frequently as sales and purchases.

   A. True
   B. False

(3) Low productivity and inefficiency seem to occur more in operations paying lower-than-average wages relative to competitors in their market area.

   A. True
   B. False

(4) Your most productive employees should be your highest-paid employees.

   A. True
   B. False

(5) Paying higher-than-average wages to your employees will increase their job performance and productivity.

   A. True
   B. False

ANSWERS: 1: A, 2: B, 3: A, 4: A, 5: B

You can be short-staffed even with the proper number of employees on the schedule

SCHEDULING IS NOT JUST A SIMPLE numbers game that requires us to match the number of employees with customer counts. While we can develop scheduling standards that would indicate that for every 100 customers we must schedule a certain number of employees at each position, it would not be effective because other considerations have to be included.

I recall giving an assistant manager the task of scheduling servers for Mother's Day, one of the biggest sales days of the year. That was my day to work, so I asked him to schedule seven waiters, one more than we normally used on busy Friday and Saturday nights. When I went to pull the guest checks for the servers and assign table stations, I glanced at the schedule the assistant manager had written and realized I was in for a long day. Included were

"I start with the premise that the function of leadership is to produce more leaders, not more followers."

— RALPH NADER

---

three rookies, who were not yet ready to handle a full station and deliver the qualitative level of service we needed to provide.

In addition to the number of customers, a schedule must take into consideration such factors as the skill and ability of each employee, the meal period, the number of tables and seats in a station, and the table-turnover rate. One example might show that a typical meal period is six hours long, the dining room has 40 tables and 160 seats, and an average of 130 seats are occupied when all tables are filled. Each server is assigned a five-to-six table station and is expected to serve 40 to 50 covers over the course of the shift. In that case the manager might determine that seven experienced waiters will be able to meet both the quantitative and qualitative aspects of service.

When scheduling, the manager must assign the right employee to the right time slot and position. To accomplish that, a manager must know the abilities and limitations of each employee. Like a baseball or basketball coach, a restaurant manager seeks to put the best employees in their positions during a busy shift. You probably recall many days when you had to struggle through a meal period with a weak cook, dishwasher, bartender or server. You weren't shorthanded in terms of the number of employees, but you were understaffed because the personnel you had working could not deliver the standards of service and preparation in a timely and efficient manner.

The skills and capabilities of each employee must be examined when maximum productivity is required. Servers are notorious for complaining about their station assignments. Certain tables and stations are considered better than others, and they usually are assigned to the senior employees. I was challenged at a staff meeting about my station assignments, and, against my better judgment, agreed to rotate stations randomly. But after struggling through a busy night in which the table turnover was reduced considerably, I returned to scheduling by employee ability. I learned that all employees are not equal in ability, speed, and efficiency, regardless of training and tenure. I needed to assign employees to areas where they could do their best. Customer service takes precedence over server-station assignment equity because you need to assess the *qualitative* aspects of the work performed as well as the *quantitative ones*. A fast cook who makes a lot of mistakes and sends out unattractive-looking food fails on the qualitative measures; by the same token the cook who turns out perfectly plated food but takes too long doesn't meet the quantitative standards.

The physical layout of the restaurant must influence scheduling as well. One factor that can have considerable impact on scheduling is the distance of the dining room from the kitchen and the bar. The greater the distance, the more time it will take to retrieve drinks and food and reduce one's ability to serve more tables and guests. Regardless of the total number of covers served during a meal period, a restaurant only can serve what the seat and table turnover will allow. The physical limitations caused by the number of tables, seats, and the length of time it takes for a customer to be seated, to order, be served, eat, and pay will all influence the number of servers needed.

When scheduling, you must also take into account the duties and responsibilities of each of your employees. Other questions that might be asked when you are scheduling servers include: Do servers have to bus and set their tables? Is there a salad bar where patrons serve themselves? Are servers required to plate and dress salads? And the same fundamental idea holds true for the other employees — the more each one is required to do, the fewer customers he or she will be able to handle. That's why you cannot use scheduling guidelines from another operation or impose purely quantitative standards.

14

Efficient scheduling requires that you monitor your business activity by the hour

SCHEDULING IS COMPLICATED because business activity fluctuates from extremely slow periods to those that are frantically busy. Scheduling would be easy if customers arrived and departed in a steady pattern. At the same time the length of an employee's shift depends on a restaurant's operating hours. Ideally, the hours of operation should be established according to customer patterns. But that's not always possible, as is illustrated by lodging foodservice operations, which may be required to run 24 hours a day.

Monitor the times during the meal period that customers enter your operation by asking a host or hostess to note the time each party is seated or when their names are placed on a waiting list. Orders also can be timed when they are turned in to the kitchen. Point-of-sale regis-

> **"When you hire people that are smarter than you are, you prove you are smarter than they are."**
>
> — R.H. GRANT

ters automatically indicate the time an order is entered into the system — information that also can reveal an operation's peak times. Plot that information on a graph showing the hours of operation to determine the peaks and valleys of customer arrivals and departures.

The arrival and departure of employees should correspond to the volume of customers expected; consequently, the maximum number of labor hours should be scheduled during the peak periods and minimum labor hours during the slow periods. That is referred to as *staggered arrivals and departure scheduling*.

When an operation is open for two or more consecutive meal periods, the changing of shifts must take place with the minimum interruption to customer service. In most restaurants employees are required to complete side work before timing out. Ideally, they should clock out exactly at the end of their scheduled shifts. However, many times they remain on the clock past their scheduled departure times because they're preparing food, cleaning up, or finishing their side work.

That can be reduced greatly or eliminated altogether through the use of a "spanner shift" employee. The schedule of a spanner employee "spans" two consecutive shifts — the end of one and the beginning of the other. For example, if the lunch shift ends at 4:00 P.M., one employee might be scheduled to clock in at 3:00 P.M. He or she relieves the departing employees so that they can finish service and complete cleanup and sidework.

When forecasts of customer counts are not accurate, management must be able to adjust man hours up or down as required. For those temporary, unpredictable periods of time, management can use an "on-call" schedule and "send home early" practices. If employees are regularly called in or sent home, the permanent schedule should reflect that procedure. Of course, local wage practices, union, and corporate policy determine whether those scheduling practices are practical. Remember: Such techniques involve only "variable cost" employees. If neither of those methods can be employed to help scheduling efficiency, marketing strategies — early-bird specials, happy hours, or discounts, for example — must be used to increase customer counts and increase sales.

(1) It is possible to be short-staffed with the proper number of employees scheduled for a particular shift.
  A. True
  B. False

(2) When scheduling employees, management must assume that all workers are equally productive in their respective jobs.
  A. True
  B. False

(3) Which of the following factors would not be a consideration in determining the number of servers to schedule and assigning stations on a busy night?
  A. The number of tables/seats a server can maintain at the service-level standard
  B. The distance of the kitchen and/or bar from the dining room
  C. The particular stations each server would "prefer" to work

(4) The arrival and departure times of employees corresponding to the volume of customers expected over the meal period is called "staggered arrival and departure scheduling."
  A. True
  B. False

(5) You actually can reduce your labor costs by giving employees a meal and break.
  A. True
  B. False

ANSWERS: 1: A, 2: B, 3: C, 4: A, 5: A

It is better to start off scheduling too few employees than too many

HAVE YOU EVER HEARD of Parkinson's Law? It's a theory that states: "Work expands to the amount of time allowed to complete it." If you give someone two hours to complete a task that could have been accomplished in one hour, they will take two hours to complete it. I would like to add another part to Parkinson's Law: "If you assign two people to do a job that one can do, they will divide the work between them."

You're always better off to begin with more restricted time frames and increased workloads than vice versa. If your employees have been practicing Parkinson's Law, they probably will resist when you shorten the time or remove their assistant. If an operation has been overstaffed for a long time, employees most likely have lowered their own productive output and will be reluctant to increase their efforts — especially if their supervisor remains the same. In some instances a management change is required to increase productivity in old employees.

Few employees are receptive to increasing their work effort. Physical and mental fatigue develop, and extra steps and motions become habitual — as when an employee walks into the dish room for clean spoons and cups and returns with only what he or she needs instead of a full tray. Side work also is procrastinated, and housekeeping standards actually slip when employees have too much time on their hands. They develop a "no need to hurry" attitude because nothing is pressing them to work faster or conserve steps. Morale falls too because management is always on their case about standing around.

The actual level of productivity of most restaurant workers never comes close to their true capabilities, but they still complain when asked to do more. Some of the bad habits they develop even may prevent them from improving their productivity. In addition, having too much time or manpower to complete a task contributes to inefficiencies because employees tend to slow down and develop an unhurried attitude, even during rush periods.

Consequently, begin by staffing lean. Later, if you find that employees are working at close to maximum productivity and still falling behind on qualitative and quantitative standards, you can schedule more employees.

Turnover happens!

KEY

16

TURNOVER IS A FACT OF LIFE in the restaurant business. Because many of the employees we hire
are entering the work force for the first time, it
is inevitable that most of them will leave within
the first six months. While we must increase the
tenure of hired workers, consider the problem
of the longtime employee who begins to resist
change and act as if he or she is not subject to
the same rules as the rest of the staff.

When changes are being made constantly,
as is often the case in developing concepts,
many times it is the employees with the longest
tenure who complain the most about having
their duties and responsibilities expanded.
Contrast that with the new hires who accept their
newly acquired job responsibility without question. Because the more senior employees exert
some informal influence over the newer employ-

> **"As a manager, the important thing is not what happens when you are there, but what happens when you are not there."**
>
> — KEN BLANCHARD

---

ees, care must be taken to ensure their reluctant attitudes are not passed on to the new hires.

I recall when my two most senior waiters told me they wanted to have a meeting after the restaurant closed for the night. As it turned out, they wanted to discuss their dissatisfaction with the additional new task of vacuuming the carpet as part of the closing waiters' duties. The job previously had been the responsibility of the night clean-up crew, which had been eliminated to cut costs. I responded by telling those two gentlemen that we needed their cooperation, but if they couldn't give it, I sadly would interpret it as their resignations.

In another situation a veteran waitress and cook had seen many assistant managers come and go, and the pair really presented a challenge to anyone assigned to that position. They took orders only from a manager who was one of the owner's relatives, which created problems when he wasn't in the restaurant. The waitress came to believe that she had her "own" station and that whenever she worked, she worked that station. The cook was equally belligerent and openly would defy the younger assistant managers. Together, they created a real management morale problem, and the other employees noticed that the pair were not held to the same standard as the new hires.

As general manager, I was informed of that situation and dealt with it accordingly. After meeting with the owner and the unit manger, we made it clear to both of those longtime employees that they were expected to follow the rules and regulations like any other employee. And if they chose not to, they would be subject to appropriate management response, which could range from being sent home, removed from the schedule, or even suspended. Once they realized that we supported the assistant manager, they become more cooperative.

One of the worst things you can do to your customers and productive employees is to retain a bad employee for too long. The old adage that "a bad apple can spoil the whole barrel" applies to how your employees deal with change. If you're not making changes in the way you operate, you're not improving and growing. Richard Melman, the founder of Lettuce Entertain You Enterprises, told a group of managers at a recent National Restaurant Association show that it's a company philosophy to make at least one change each month in all of his restaurants. That change may be a different ingredient in a recipe, a different supplier, a new menu item, or even just a change in the way napkins are folded. Change sends a signal to management and employees that the operation continually is trying to improve.

(1) When an operation has been overstaffed for a prolonged period of time, employees will decrease their output and be reluctant to increase their efforts.

    A. True
    B. False

(2) The actual level of productivity of most restaurant workers is very close to their maximum capabilities.

    A. True
    B. False

(3) Having too much time or manpower to complete a task contributes to inefficiencies in performance and productivity.

    A. True
    B. False

(4) Making small but noticeable changes in the way you conduct your business sends a signal that the operation is continually trying to improve.

    A. True
    B. False

(5) A low labor-cost percentage is an accurate indication of high productivity and efficiency.

    A. True
    B. False

ANSWERS: 1: A, 2: B, 3: A, 4: A, 5: B

17

The manager remains the key element in improving employee productivity

THE IMPORTANCE OF MANAGEMENT in controlling labor cost and increasing productivity cannot be overstated. Labor-cost control begins with proper hiring, training, and supervision. Much of the attitude, ability, and professionalism of a manager is reflected in the type of employees hired, trained, and retained. It's imperative that management inform the employees right from the start what is expected of them in terms of attitude and performance.

A manager must be able to explain the reason for procedures to keep employees from taking short cuts that lower standards. Explaining the "why" of procedures and standards helps develop values and positive attitudes in employees. A conscious effort must be made to enforce standards and monitor employee performance. Employees need objective measurements to guide them so that they can keep score of their own performance.

Highly productive and service-minded employees do not come to be that way on their own; they are a product of their work environment. Managers always have earned their pay by doing the best they can with the human and physical resources available to them. No manager ever had everything that he or she wanted in the way of budget, staff, location, equipment, or product mix. And it's getting even more difficult to field a competitive team as the demand for employees grows faster than the supply.

If management allows standards to slip or accepts less than the standard, it will become more difficult to achieve standards in the future. Remember: Employees will deviate from standards only as far as management allows. Follow-up meetings and appraisals are necessary to implant standards in employees' minds.

Like a coach, the manager motivates the employee team. As management goes, so goes the restaurant. Systematic evaluation of an employee's job performance is essential to measure progress in the development of job skills; to identify substandard performance and to correct it; and to provide the basis for recognition, promotion, and merit-wage increases.

18

Don't overlook the improvement in productivity that can result from using labor-saving equipment, improving layout, and outsourcing a task

PRODUCTIVITY CAN BE INCREASED by the use of labor-saving equipment, improved layout and design of the workplace, or elimination of a task or the need for scheduling an employee by out-sourcing the activity. The purchase of automatic equipment often can lead to a reduction in the number of labor hours scheduled. For example, if you remodel the dish room and install a more efficient dish machine, and, at the same time, increase the inventory of china, glassware, and silver, you probably could reduce the number of employees required during peak periods.

If $10,000 in capital expenditures resulted in the elimination of just one employee earning a minimum wage of $10,712 annually, a savings of over $712 would be realized the first year. The actual annual savings would be hundreds

> **"Many of us have heard opportunity knocking at our door, but by the time we unhooked the chain, pushed back the bolt, turned two locks, and shut off the burglar alarm — it was gone."**
>
> — ANONYMOUS

---

of dollars more and would include savings from nonpayment of employee meals, uniforms, benefits, and payroll taxes.

In the food-preparation area, the investment in equipment and labor could be eliminated if food items were purchased premade. For example, few operations can afford the investment in space, equipment, and manpower to have an in-house bakery. Therefore, they purchase breads, cakes, and pies from outside suppliers. While the raw food cost of the prepared items is higher than if they were made in-house, the operations don't have to invest in equipment, space, or labor. In addition, the bulk ingredients required for in-house baking don't have to be carried in inventory.

If the space and equipment were already in place, cost savings still could be achieved by preparing only certain items in-house and purchasing the remainder from outside sources.

That would reduce the number of total labor hours scheduled and result in lower payroll costs. And if full-time employees could be replaced by part-time employees, further savings could result.

Some of the labor required in the dining room can be transferred to the customer in the form of self-service. Many fast-food restaurants are placing beverage stations in the dining area for customers to help themselves. While those operations might experience a slight increase in product cost because of free refills and sharing by customers, the savings in labor more than offsets any increase.

At the same time drive-through windows are allowing more customers to be served by fewer employees. The amount of sales that pass through the drive-through more than offsets the cost of the labor of the window-person. The increased business levels sparked by such service-delivery systems as drive-through windows, delivery, and carryout have been made possible by improved organization of the work area and the incorporation of electronic communication systems and labor-saving equipment.

The automatic-portion dispensers now installed on soft-drink fountains allow the employee to press a button and automatically portion the proper amount of soda without having to hold down the lever. Consequently, employees are free to walk over to the french fry station and pick up their order. That action may take only five seconds, but it can add up to many minutes when repeated hundreds of times over an eight-hour shift.

Any time you can eliminate a bottleneck in the flow of work that allows product to reach the customer faster, you will save time and money and provide better service to your customers. If you develop systems that enable your employees to achieve the qualitative and quantitative standards in the delivery of service and preparation of food and beverages, the customer is better served.

19

Understaffing can cause problems both with employee morale and customer service

CONTROLLING LABOR COST presents the biggest challenge that a restaurant manager faces on a daily basis. More managers are terminated because of their inability to deal with employees than for their inability to control food or beverage costs. While payroll percentages look good when you're operating short-handed, they have more serious negative consequences if they're not addressed within a reasonable time.

Your hardest-working and most productive employees probably are asked to work longer hours and, as a result, must endure the stress of a work environment where they never seem to be in control. Even those loyal employees eventually will lose their incentive if they have to work harder and longer because the operation is understaffed. You have to recognize these employees as being special, treat them with respect, and show your appreciation. Imagine how it would be if they weren't there during tough times.

I have a renewed appreciation and respect for those productive employees in the dish room, on the cooking line, in the dining room, and in the bar. Over the Christmas holidays I worked a couple of nights in a friend's restaurant because the operation was short-handed. I saw and felt how stressful it was for everyone because we couldn't perform up to standards. Food came out slowly, mistakes were made on orders, and customers received the wrong food or food that hadn't been cooked properly. Newly hired servers — panic-hires without proper training — who didn't know how to ring up orders or couldn't answer questions about menu items were turned loose on the floor.

At the same time senior employees were getting stressed out because they couldn't get their food and drinks fast enough to develop a rhythm for serving customers efficiently. Their morale was suffering too. Furthermore, quality ingredients were ruined by cooks who fell behind and were forced to take shortcuts just to get the food out. The owner admonished employees when they made a mistake or moved too slowly. Although we were doing the best we could given our lack of knowledge, the quality standards were not being maintained. That experience reminded me how important confident and competent employees are in maintaining your service and food quality standards. If they don't have the confidence in themselves, they will not have a positive attitude about their job.

20

Use breaks and meal credits to help reduce your overall payroll costs

DO YOU PROVIDE A MEAL for your employees when they work a full shift? Do you take a wage credit for the fair cost of that meal against their hourly wage? Do you give your employees a 30-minute break during their shift? If you answered no, you possibly can save on your payroll by adopting those measures. If the answer is yes, but you have not been deducting 30 minutes off their time or utilizing the meal credit to which you are legally entitled, you are spending money that you could be saving.

Under the Wage and Hour Law, an employer can take a credit against the hourly wage for the cost of a meal offered to employees at no charge. The amount of the credit must reflect the reasonable cost of the food. The credit is prorated on an hourly basis. As an example, assume an employee is paid $5.15 per hour and works an average of eight hours per day. The total daily wage rate would be $41.20. Assume further that the employee is given a free meal that has a reasonable cost of $2.00. A credit against the hourly wage can be claimed in the amount of 25 cents per hour, or $2.00 divided by eight hours. Therefore, the hourly wage would be reduced from $5.15 to $4.90.

In addition, if the employee is given a 30-minute break to eat, he or she will be paid for seven and a half hours rather than the full eight. The daily compensation would be reduced from $41.20 to $36.75. If you employ 25 people, the savings would amount to over $40,495 per year. Why not utilize the deductions that are yours for the taking?

21

You cannot make an unproductive employee productive by simply paying him more money

WHICH COMES FIRST: the pay increase or the increase in productivity? Put another way, which comes first: the raise or the effort that deserves a raise? You know the answer, but let me relate a story about the marginal employee who asks his manager for a raise after being on the job for six months. This employee comes to work every day, does what he is required to do, doesn't make trouble, and follows most of the rules. He tells the manager that if he were to receive another 50 cents an hour, he would work twice as hard and twice as fast as he had in the past.

When we reward employees for doing the fundamental things, it's like recommending a restaurant because it's clean and has good food and friendly service. Like the employee's evaluation, those basic things should be viewed as

> **"We herd sheep, we drive cattle, we lead people. Lead me, follow me, or get out of my way."**
>
> — GEORGE S. PATTON

---

implicit, not extra or special. But business is so competitive today that an employee who does his or her job and doesn't cause problems probably would stand out and very likely be rewarded with a raise.

I remember something that my favorite college professor, the late Peter Dukas, told us in class. He said, "Identifying with ownership interests is the quickest way to be recognized for advancement." If you can think like an owner, you will perform differently and your attitude will change. Look for the employees who are willing to do more and take greater responsibility. They are the ones who deserve the raises.

We cannot adjust our productivity to our pay scale because we are all basically underpaid. If we attempt to adjust our workload to reflect that fact, productivity never would improve. We're still impressed by the employee who accepts more responsibility than his or her job description requires. We're also impressed by the employee who is willing to work whenever and wherever needed. However, if that kind of effort goes unnoticed and unrewarded by management, that employee will either quit or eventually stop doing extra work because there is no incentive to do so.

If the payment of more money to an employee guaranteed higher productivity, I doubt that anyone in our industry would be against increasing the minimum wage. The reason we're against it is that we're compelled to pay the unproductive employees a wage that we've been paying our more productive ones. That forces us to ensure that all employees are productive and that we're not scheduling people, but purchasing the potential to do work.

While it's true that high wages and high productivity don't always follow, money is still an effective reward for outstanding performance and loyalty. But raises and bonuses cannot be doled out according to seniority and not performance. If that's the case, then hard-working employees are being short-changed. If everyone receives the same bonus, it devalues the bonus in the minds of the employees who have done more than their share. Those employees who go beyond the normal scope of their duties should be rewarded at a higher level than others who simply do what they were hired to do and nothing more.

The American way is to prove your worth to your employer first and be rewarded afterward. And if you feel guilty about what you're paying a worker because he or she is hard working and dedicated, that worker probably deserves a raise.

(1) You can tell a lot about a manager by looking at the type of employees that are hired, trained, and retained.

A. True
B. False

(2) Employees need only to be told "what" to do. It is not necessary to explain "why."

A. True
B. False

(3) Management cannot control how much employees deviate from prescribed standards.

A. True
B. False

(4) Labor-saving equipment can lead to a reduction in the number of labor hours scheduled.

A. True
B. False

(5) More managers lose their jobs because of their inability to deal with employees and labor cost than their inability to control food or beverage costs.

A. True
B. False

ANSWERS: 1: A, 2: B, 3: B, 4: A, 5: A

22

Productivity can be improved by utilizing unused employee capacity

ONE WAY TO INCREASE PRODUCTIVITY and maximize the same amount of labor hours is to identify *unused employee capacity*. Full-time employees who are clocked in and waiting for their main duties to begin result in unused employee capacity. While the scheduling of part-time employees can reduce the number of total labor hours, full-time employees must be scheduled for 40 hours per week; consequently, management must keep them busy and productive. Nonproductive, wasted hours should be reduced either by removing those workers from the schedule or by utilizing them in some capacity when they are on the clock.

One solution is to cross-train employees to do more than just the duties of the primary job description. The employees that cannot be sent home during idle time should be assigned other activities that will allow you to reduce the total labor hours scheduled. For example, ask a properly trained server to bartend during a rush; train a dishwasher to do prep work before the lunch rush; schedule an assistant manager to work the cooking line for an hour or two during peak periods. All of those measures will increase output without increasing input and/or labor costs.

But be careful: If productive employees are given additional work once they've finished their assigned tasks while others continue to take their time, they too eventually will practice Parkinson's Law.

And don't forget that restaurants must schedule a minimum number of employees whenever they're open. That fixed labor cannot be reduced, even when sales fluctuate downward. That's why the labor-cost percentage increases when sales decrease. It's an undeniable fact of the business that we're labor intensive, and for that reason the restaurant business will never be as productive as the more capital-intensive businesses in the manufacturing sector. Because we're a service industry, machines and improved layouts cannot replace the human element, especially in the customer-service areas.

23

Labor productivity must address both qualitative and quantitative factors

IMPROVING LABOR PRODUCTIVITY is accomplished either by performing more work with the same number of employees working the same number of hours, or by performing the same amount of work with fewer people or in less time. However, if the quality of your food product and customer service declines in the process, you have harmed and not helped your operation.

Productivity involves anything that affects your restaurant's ability to produce menu items and provide quality service to your customers. It includes both behavioral and technical components, such as the motivation of employees and the utilization of labor-saving equipment.

When you attempt to accomplish more with fewer resources and less manpower, your operation may fail to meet its qualitative stan-

"Leadership: The art of getting someone else to do something you want done because he wants to do it."

— DWIGHT D. EISENHOWER

---

dards. And if you do succeed in increasing productivity at the expense of quality standards, you have created a serious problem for yourself. However, there's so much room for increasing productivity that you shouldn't really encounter a problem unless you reduce staffing to the bare bones.

Training and labor-saving devices can help you increase productivity by raising the output of individual employees. By taking that route, the quality of service should improve also. Even marketing strategy can raise productivity. Increasing customer counts and the volume of business activity can result in marked reduction in labor-cost percentages, lower labor cost per customer, and a higher number of transactions per labor hour. Nevertheless, if that succeeds in increasing business, management should resist the urge to add too many variable-cost employees to the schedule.

Labor cost can be held in check if the scheduling of employee tasks is managed along with the time, quantity, and quality standards. Utilizing that method, the general job description is broken down into the required specific tasks, schedules are established for those tasks, and the optimum output that should be achieved within a standard work period is determined. The tasks described can be as simple as rolling silverware in napkins or completing a sales audit of all servers. The key to task analysis is to determine achievable workloads for each task through detailed measurement.

Essentially, a productivity-improvement program involves the setting of standards and goals and then the monitoring of performance. Productivity encompasses everything that affects your restaurant's ability to produce goods and services and everything that affects the demand for those goods and services. In addition, anything that improves efficiency will help improve productivity. So it should be clear that enhancing productivity is not just a matter of leaner scheduling; productivity can be improved by training, labor-saving equipment, improved layout and design, an increase in business volume, or an increase in the average check. But remember: The most important factor in the productivity equation is smart management.

(1) One way to improve productivity is to cross-train employees so they can be kept busy when they are not engaged in their primary duties.

    A. True
    B. False

(2) The primary tool for controlling labor costs is:

    A. Paying help what the "market will bear" in hourly wages
    B. Scheduling help efficiently
    C. Paying as close to the minimum wage as possible

(3) Most inefficiencies in scheduling employees occurs with "fixed-cost" employees.

    A. True
    B. False

(4) Enhancing productivity is only a matter of scheduling fewer employees.

    A. True
    B. False

(5) Productivity involves anything that improves your restaurant's ability to produce menu items and provide quality service to your customers.

    A. True
    B. False

ANSWERS: 1: A, 2: B, 3: B, 4: B, 5: A

24

If you reduce employee turnover and increase retention, productivity will improve

WORKER PRODUCTIVITY in the restaurant industry is about half of that of workers in the manufacturing industries. However, there are some logical reasons for that. The restaurant industry takes raw product, processes it, and makes the finished product available to the customers on the same premises. Product demand has daily peaks in the selling cycle. The finished product cannot be stockpiled for long, and final inspection is conducted by the consumer. Furthermore, a restaurant is part of a labor-intensive service industry that cannot substitute machines for manpower.

In times of need restaurateurs often find themselves facing the prospects of "panic hiring" — in other words, having to scramble to fill positions with warm bodies because they don't have the time to hire properly. In fact, they may have been running an ad for several weeks without any viable applicants applying or calling.

I recall a personnel director of a national restaurant chain say that if his chain could increase the tenure of its hourly employees by just 60 days, labor costs could be reduced by 20 percent. Management must focus its attention on the reasons why employees quit. They can do little or nothing about personal problems, family issues, or those employees who move out of the area. But exit interviews must be conducted to discover if something in the work environment is contributing to turnover.

Good employees are getting more difficult to find. Therefore, when you find them, do everything you can to keep them. It starts with letting them know that they are valued individuals — and valued individuals are paid well and shown that they are appreciated in many other ways. You must have the right people on the right job at the right time. Once you have found them, do everything in your power to keep them.

Once labor costs have been cut to the bare bones, only an increase in sales can lower the payroll percentage

REMEMBER: COST REDUCTION is only one strategy for improving your bottom line. Low costs by themselves do not result in a solvent and profitable operation. Many managers are great at controlling costs, but their operations are not really thriving in the financial sense. When costs are under control and have been pared to the bare bones, the only way to improve profit is to increase sales.

Consequently, your overall business plan must include a marketing strategy. You must bring in customers, and that takes advertising and promotion. Nothing is more discouraging to a manager who has his costs under control than not having the sales volume to optimize profit. Morale will begin to flag. The situation is analogous to that of an athletic coach who drills his team every day to prepare them for the big

> **"If we don't change, we don't grow. If we don't grow, we aren't really living."**
>
> — GAIL SHEEHY

game on Friday night — only to have the game canceled every week.

It becomes harder and harder for employees to maintain their edge and confidence if the business volume never improves. They begin to question whether it's worth the time and effort they must expend. They never really get to "do their thing" on a busy night. And since only increased sales can make that happen, part of your overall business strategy must be focused on achieving that end.

(1) The productivity of the average foodservice worker is about double the productivity of workers in the manufacturing industries.
   A. True
   B. False

(2) Increasing the tenure of hourly workers by just 60 days would reduce overall labor costs by approximately 20 percent.
   A. True
   B. False

(3) Low costs by themselves do not result in a solvent and profitable operation.
   A. True
   B. False

(4) Once costs have been pared to the bare bones, the only way to increase profit is to increase sales.
   A. True
   B. False

(5) In order to schedule the proper number of employees, all management needs to know is the forecasted number of customers for the period being scheduled.
   A. True
   B. False

ANSWERS: 1: B, 2: A, 3: A, 4: A, 5: B

DAVE PAVESIC is a former restaurateur who now teaches hospitality administration at the university level. He previously owned and operated two casual-theme Italian restaurants in Orlando, Fla.; served as general manager of operations of a six-unit regional chain in the Midwest, operating four coffee shops, a fine-dining seafood restaurant and one drive-in; and was a college foodservice director. He currently teaches courses on restaurant cost control, financial management, and food production in the Cecil B. Day School of Hospitality Administration at Georgia State University in Atlanta, Ga. He has written numerous articles on menu-sales analysis, labor cost, menu pricing and equipment layout. His two other books are *The Fundamental Principles of Restaurant Cost Control*, Prentice Hall Publishers, 1998, ISBN 0-13-747999-9 and *Menu Pricing and Strategy*, fourth edition, Van Nostrand Reinhold Publishers, 1996, ISBN 0-471-28747-4.